Change Your Name Change The Game

Accept • Become • Create

Dear Rockstar:

It is truly an honor to play a part in Your name change. A name change that will take You to places You have never imagined. I am so proud of this new bold move You are making for You.

When we came into this world, we took on so many different identities that we forgot who we really are. However, things are about to shift because You are changing your name, which will in turn change the game. We are always one decision away from changing the rest of our lives.

As you begin your new journey, let's affirm that we **accept** what is, we commit to **become** our truest selves, which will allow us to **create** the life of our wildest dreams! It's as easy as ABC!

Accept:

We accept the choices we have made up until now. We forgive ourselves and we unconditionally love the identity that has led us to this point in time. We understand that we did the best that we knew how with the information that we had.

Become:

We now decide to become one with our true identity. We fully embrace who we really are, and when we forget, we lovingly remind ourselves to return home. We allow our lives to unfold right before our eyes without judgment or condemnation.

Create:

We believe that we create our realities. We now exercise our freedom to make decisions that support the vision that we have for our lives. We surrender our thoughts and beliefs to the Christ Mind within, and we expect our manifestations to be exceeding abundantly above what we ask or think, according to the power that works in us.

I created this Workbook as a pocket journal for you to use as a tool to remind yourself of who You really are. You are whole, worthy, excellent, loving, abundant, brave and bold!

Your a game changer!

Let the games begin!

Best,

Andrenee

I am Whole

I now release any and all thoughts, beliefs and feelings about my life that are not in alignment with my Wholeness and surrender them to the Presence of God in me.

	OLD	NEW
THOUGHTS		
BELIEFS		
FEELINGS		
ACTIONS		
SUMMARY		

be whole today

❤ DATE

❤ THINGS TO DO

❤ SCHEDULE FOR TODAY

1 ....

2 ....

3 ....

4 ....

5 ....

6 ....

❤ NOTES

LIVE SIMPLY. DREAM BIG. BE GRATEFUL. LAUGH LOTS.

ANDRENEE'S CORNER, LLC

CERTIFICATE OF WHOLENESS

This certificate is presented to

Sign Your Name

for having the courage to change your name and giving yourself permission to be the Perfect, Whole and Complete Being God created You to be!

Presented by: Andrenee Boothe, CEO & Founder

I am Worthy

I now release any and all thoughts, beliefs and feelings about my life that are not in alignment with my Worthiness and surrender them to the Presence of God in me.

	OLD	NEW
THOUGHTS		
BELIEFS		
FEELINGS ,		
ACTIONS		
SUMMARY		

be worthy today

♥ **DATE**

♥ **SCHEDULE FOR TODAY**

1 ....

2 ....

3 ....

4 ....

5 ....

6 ....

♥ **THINGS TO DO**

♥ **NOTES**

LIVE SIMPLY. DREAM BIG. BE GRATEFUL. LAUGH LOTS.

ANDRENEE'S CORNER, LLC

CERTIFICATE OF WORTHINESS

This certificate is presented to

Sign Your Name

for having the courage to change your name and giving yourself permission to be the Worthy Being God created You to be!

Presented by: Andrenee Boothe, CEO & Founder

I am Excellence

I now release any and all thoughts, beliefs and feelings about my life that are not in alignment with my Excellence and surrender them to the Presence of God in me.

	OLD	NEW
THOUGHTS		
BELIEFS		
FEELINGS		
ACTIONS		
SUMMARY		

be excellent today

♥ **DATE**

♥ **THINGS TO DO**

♥ **SCHEDULE FOR TODAY**

1 ....
2 ....
3 ....
4 ....
5 ....
6 ....

♥ **NOTES**

LIVE SIMPLY. DREAM BIG. BE GRATEFUL. LAUGH LOTS.

ANDRENEE'S CORNER, LLC

CERTIFICATE OF EXCELLENCE

This certificate is presented to

Sign Your Name

for having the courage to change your name and giving
yourself permission to be the Excellent Leader God
created You to be!

Presented by: Andrenee Boothe, CEO & Founder

I am Love

I now release any and all thoughts, beliefs and feelings about my life that are not in alignment with Love and surrender them to the Presence of God in me.

	OLD	NEW
THOUGHTS		
BELIEFS		
FEELINGS		
ACTIONS		
SUMMARY		

be loving today

♥ **DATE**

♥ **THINGS TO DO**

♥ **SCHEDULE FOR TODAY**

1 ....

2 ....

3 ....

4 ....

5 ....

6 ....

♥ **NOTES**

ANDRENEE'S CORNER, LLC

CERTIFICATE OF COMPASSION

This certificate is presented to

Sign Your Name

for having the courage to change your name and giving yourself permission to be the Loving Being God created You to be!

Presented by: Andrenee Boothe, CEO & Founder

I am Abundant

I now release any and all thoughts, beliefs and feelings about my life that are not in alignment with my Abundance and surrender them to the Presence of God in me.

	OLD	NEW
THOUGHTS		
BELIEFS		
FEELINGS		
ACTIONS		
SUMMARY		

be abundant today

♥ **DATE**

♥ **SCHEDULE FOR TODAY**

1 ....

2 ....

3 ....

4 ....

5 ....

6 ....

♥ **THINGS TO DO**

♥ **NOTES**

LIVE SIMPLY. DREAM BIG. BE GRATEFUL. LAUGH LOTS.

ANDRENEE'S CORNER, LLC

CERTIFICATE OF PROSPERITY

This certificate is presented to

Sign Your Name

*for having the courage to change your name and giving
yourself permission to be the Abundant Being God
created You to be!*

Presented by: Andrenee Boothe, CEO & Founder

I am Brave

I now release any and all thoughts, beliefs and feelings about my life that are not in alignment with my Courage and surrender them to the Presence of God in me.

	OLD	NEW
THOUGHTS		
BELIEFS		
FEELINGS		
ACTIONS		
SUMMARY		

be brave today

♥ **DATE**

♥ **SCHEDULE FOR TODAY**

1 ....

2 ....

3 ....

4 ....

5 ....

6 ....

♥ **THINGS TO DO**

♥ **NOTES**

LIVE SIMPLY. DREAM BIG. BE GRATEFUL. LAUGH LOTS.

ANDRENEE'S CORNER, LLC

CERTIFICATE OF BRAVERY

This certificate is presented to

Sign Your Name

for having the courage to change your name and giving yourself permission to be the Risk Taking Leader God created You to be!

Presented by: Andrenee Boothe, CEO & Founder

I am Daring

I now release any and all thoughts, beliefs and feelings about my life that are not in alignment with my Audaciousness and surrender them to the Presence of God in me.

	OLD	NEW
THOUGHTS		
BELIEFS		
FEELINGS		
ACTIONS		
SUMMARY		

be daring today

♥ **DATE**

♥ **SCHEDULE FOR TODAY**

1 ....

2 ....

3 ....

4 ....

5 ....

6 ....

♥ **THINGS TO DO**

♥ **NOTES**

CERTIFICATE OF BOLDNESS

This certificate is presented to

Sign Your Name

for having the courage to change your name and giving
yourself permission to be the Bold Leader God
created You to be!

Presented by: Andrenee Boothe, CEO & Founder

I am Whole

I now release any and all thoughts, beliefs and feelings about my life that are not in alignment with my Wholeness and surrender them to the Presence of God in me.

	OLD	NEW
THOUGHTS		
BELIEFS		
FEELINGS		
ACTIONS		
SUMMARY		

be whole today

♥ **DATE**

♥ **THINGS TO DO**

♥ **SCHEDULE FOR TODAY**

1 ....

2 ....

3 ....

4 ....

5 ....

6 ....

♥ **NOTES**

LIVE SIMPLY. DREAM BIG. BE GRATEFUL. LAUGH LOTS.

ANDRENEE'S CORNER, LLC

CERTIFICATE OF WHOLENESS

This certificate is presented to

Sign Your Name

for having the courage to change your name and giving yourself permission to be the Perfect, Whole and Complete Being God created You to be!

Presented by: Andrenee Boothe, CEO & Founder

I am Worthy

I now release any and all thoughts, beliefs and feelings about my life that are not in alignment with my Worthiness and surrender them to the Presence of God in me.

	OLD	NEW
THOUGHTS		
BELIEFS		
FEELINGS		
ACTIONS		
SUMMARY		

be worthy today

♥ **DATE**

♥ **SCHEDULE FOR TODAY**

1 ....
2 ....
3 ....
4 ....
5 ....
6 ....

♥ **THINGS TO DO**

♥ **NOTES**

LIVE SIMPLY. DREAM BIG. BE GRATEFUL. LAUGH LOTS.

ANDRENEE'S CORNER, LLC

CERTIFICATE OF WORTHINESS

This certificate is presented to

Sign Your Name

for having the courage to change your name and giving
yourself permission to be the Worthy Being God
created You to be!

Presented by: Andrenee Boothe, CEO & Founder

I am Excellence

I now release any and all thoughts, beliefs and feelings about my life that are not in alignment with my Excellence and surrender them to the Presence of God in me.

	OLD	NEW
THOUGHTS		
BELIEFS		
FEELINGS		
ACTIONS		
SUMMARY		

be excellent today

♥ **DATE**

♥ **SCHEDULE FOR TODAY**

1 ....

2 ....

3 ....

4 ....

5 ....

6 ....

♥ **THINGS TO DO**

♥ **NOTES**

LIVE SIMPLY. DREAM BIG. BE GRATEFUL. LAUGH LOTS.

ANDRENEE'S CORNER, LLC

CERTIFICATE OF EXCELLENCE

This certificate is presented to

_____

Sign Your Name

for having the courage to change your name and giving yourself permission to be the Excellent Leader God created You to be!

Presented by: Andrenee Boothe, CEO & Founder

I am Love

I now release any and all thoughts, beliefs and feelings about my life that are not in alignment with Love and surrender them to the Presence of God in me.

	OLD	NEW
THOUGHTS		
BELIEFS		
FEELINGS		
ACTIONS		
SUMMARY		

be loving today

♥ **DATE**

♥ **SCHEDULE FOR TODAY**

1 ....

2 ....

3 ....

4 ....

5 ....

6 ....

♥ **THINGS TO DO**

♥ **NOTES**

LIVE SIMPLY. DREAM BIG. BE GRATEFUL. LAUGH LOTS.

ANDRENEE'S CORNER, LLC

CERTIFICATE OF COMPASSION

This certificate is presented to

Sign Your Name

for having the courage to change your name and giving
yourself permission to be the Loving Being God
created You to be!

Presented by: Andrenee Boothe, CEO & Founder

I am Abundant

I now release any and all thoughts, beliefs and feelings about my life that are not in alignment with my Abundance and surrender them to the Presence of God in me.

	OLD	NEW
THOUGHTS		
BELIEFS		
FEELINGS		
ACTIONS		
SUMMARY		

be abundant today

♥ **DATE**

♥ **THINGS TO DO**

♥ **SCHEDULE FOR TODAY**

1 ....

2 ....

3 ....

4 ....

5 ....

6 ....

♥ **NOTES**

LIVE SIMPLY. DREAM BIG. BE GRATEFUL. LAUGH LOTS.

CERTIFICATE OF PROSPERITY

ANDRENEE'S CORNER, LLC

This certificate is presented to

Sign Your Name

for having the courage to change your name and giving
yourself permission to be the Abundant Being God
created You to be!

Presented by: Andrenee Boothe, CEO & Founder

I am Brave

I now release any and all thoughts, beliefs and feelings about my life that are not in alignment with my Courage and surrender them to the Presence of God in me.

	OLD	NEW
THOUGHTS		
BELIEFS		
FEELINGS		
ACTIONS		
SUMMARY		

be brave today

♥ **DATE**

♥ **THINGS TO DO**

♥ **SCHEDULE FOR TODAY**

1 ....

2 ....

3 ....

4 ....

5 ....

6 ....

♥ **NOTES**

LIVE SIMPLY. DREAM BIG. BE GRATEFUL. LAUGH LOTS.

ANDRENEE'S CORNER, LLC

CERTIFICATE OF BRAVERY

This certificate is presented to

Sign Your Name

for having the courage to change your name and giving yourself permission to be the Risk Taking Leader God created You to be!

Presented by: Andrenee Boothe, CEO & Founder

I am Daring

I now release any and all thoughts, beliefs and feelings about my life that are not in alignment with my Audaciousness and surrender them to the Presence of God in me.

	OLD	NEW
THOUGHTS		
BELIEFS		
FEELINGS		
ACTIONS		
SUMMARY		

be daring today

♥ **DATE**

♥ **SCHEDULE FOR TODAY**

1 ....

2 ....

3 ....

4 ....

5 ....

6 ....

♥ **THINGS TO DO**

♥ **NOTES**

LIVE SIMPLY. DREAM BIG. BE GRATEFUL. LAUGH LOTS.

CERTIFICATE OF BOLDNESS

This certificate is presented to

_____

Sign Your Name

for having the courage to change your name and giving yourself permission to be the Bold Leader God created You to be!

Presented by: Andrenee Boothe, CEO & Founder

I am Whole

I now release any and all thoughts, beliefs and feelings about my life that are not in alignment with my Wholeness and surrender them to the Presence of God in me.

	OLD	NEW
THOUGHTS		
BELIEFS		
FEELINGS		
ACTIONS		
SUMMARY		

be whole today

♥ **DATE**

♥ **THINGS TO DO**

♥ **SCHEDULE FOR TODAY**

1 ....

2 ....

3 ....

4 ....

5 ....

6 ....

♥ **NOTES**

LIVE SIMPLY. DREAM BIG. BE GRATEFUL. LAUGH LOTS.

ANDRENEE'S CORNER, LLC

CERTIFICATE OF WHOLENESS

This certificate is presented to

_____

Sign Your Name

for having the courage to change your name and giving
yourself permission to be the Perfect, Whole and
Complete Being God created You to be!

Presented by: Andrenee Boothe, CEO & Founder

I am Worthy

I now release any and all thoughts, beliefs and feelings about my life that are not in alignment with my Worthiness and surrender them to the Presence of God in me.

	OLD	NEW
THOUGHTS		
BELIEFS		
FEELINGS		
ACTIONS		
SUMMARY		

be worthy today

♥ **DATE**

♥ **SCHEDULE FOR TODAY**

1 ....
2 ....
3 ....
4 ....
5 ....
6 ....

♥ **THINGS TO DO**

♥ **NOTES**

LIVE SIMPLY. DREAM BIG. BE GRATEFUL. LAUGH LOTS.

ANDRENEE'S CORNER, LLC

CERTIFICATE OF WORTHINESS

This certificate is presented to

_____

Sign Your Name

for having the courage to change your name and giving yourself permission to be the Worthy Being God created You to be!

Presented by: Andrenee Boothe, CEO & Founder

I am Excellence

I now release any and all thoughts, beliefs and feelings about my life that are not in alignment with my Excellence and surrender them to the Presence of God in me.

	OLD	NEW
THOUGHTS		
BELIEFS		
FEELINGS		
ACTIONS		
SUMMARY		

be excellent today

♥ **DATE**

♥ **SCHEDULE FOR TODAY**

1 ....
2 ....
3 ....
4 ....
5 ....
6 ....

♥ **THINGS TO DO**

♥ **NOTES**

LIVE SIMPLY. DREAM BIG. BE GRATEFUL. LAUGH LOTS.

ANDRENEE'S CORNER, LLC

CERTIFICATE OF EXCELLENCE

This certificate is presented to

Sign Your Name

for having the courage to change your name and giving
yourself permission to be the Excellent Leader God
created You to be!

Presented by: Andrenee Boothe, CEO & Founder

I am Love

I now release any and all thoughts, beliefs and feelings about my life that are not in alignment with Love and surrender them to the Presence of God in me.

	OLD	NEW
THOUGHTS		
BELIEFS		
FEELINGS		
ACTIONS		
SUMMARY		

be loving today

♥ **DATE**

♥ **SCHEDULE FOR TODAY**

1 ....

2 ....

3 ....

4 ....

5 ....

6 ....

♥ **THINGS TO DO**

♥ **NOTES**

LIVE SIMPLY. DREAM BIG. BE GRATEFUL. LAUGH LOTS.

ANDRENEE'S CORNER, LLC

CERTIFICATE OF COMPASSION

This certificate is presented to

Sign Your Name

for having the courage to change your name and giving
yourself permission to be the Loving Being God
created You to be!

Presented by: Andrenee Boothe, CEO & Founder

I am Abundant

I now release any and all thoughts, beliefs and feelings about my life that are not in alignment with my Abundance and surrender them to the Presence of God in me.

	OLD	NEW
THOUGHTS		
BELIEFS		
FEELINGS		
ACTIONS		
SUMMARY		

be abundant today

♥ DATE

♥ THINGS TO DO

♥ SCHEDULE FOR TODAY

1 ....

2 ....

3 ....

4 ....

5 ....

6 ....

♥ NOTES

ANDRENEE'S CORNER, LLC

CERTIFICATE OF PROSPERITY

This certificate is presented to

Sign Your Name

for having the courage to change your name and giving yourself permission to be the Abundant Being God created You to be!

Presented by: Andrenee Boothe, CEO & Founder

I am Brave

I now release any and all thoughts, beliefs and feelings about my life that are not in alignment with my Courage and surrender them to the Presence of God in me.

	OLD	NEW
THOUGHTS		
BELIEFS		
FEELINGS		
ACTIONS		
SUMMARY		

be brave today

♥ **DATE**

♥ **SCHEDULE FOR TODAY**

1 ....

2 ....

3 ....

4 ....

5 ....

6 ....

♥ **THINGS TO DO**

♥ **NOTES**

LIVE SIMPLY. DREAM BIG. BE GRATEFUL. LAUGH LOTS.

CERTIFICATE OF BRAVERY

This certificate is presented to

Sign Your Name

for having the courage to change your name and giving yourself permission to be the Risk Taking Leader God created You to be!

Presented by: Andrenee Boothe, CEO & Founder

I am Daring

I now release any and all thoughts, beliefs and feelings about my life that are not in alignment with my Audaciousness and surrender them to the Presence of God in me.

	OLD	NEW
THOUGHTS		
BELIEFS		
FEELINGS		
ACTIONS		
SUMMARY		

be daring today

♥ **DATE**

♥ **SCHEDULE FOR TODAY**

1 ....
2 ....
3 ....
4 ....
5 ....
6 ....

♥ **THINGS TO DO**

♥ **NOTES**

LIVE SIMPLY. DREAM BIG. BE GRATEFUL. LAUGH LOTS.

CERTIFICATE OF BOLDNESS

This certificate is presented to

Sign Your Name

for having the courage to change your name and giving yourself permission to be the Bold Leader God created You to be!

Presented by: Andrenee Boothe, CEO & Founder

I am Whole

I now release any and all thoughts, beliefs and feelings about my life that are not in alignment with my Wholeness and surrender them to the Presence of God in me.

	OLD	NEW
THOUGHTS		
BELIEFS		
FEELINGS		
ACTIONS		
SUMMARY		

be whole today

♥ **DATE**

♥ **THINGS TO DO**

♥ **SCHEDULE FOR TODAY**

1 ....
2 ....
3 ....
4 ....
5 ....
6 ....

♥ **NOTES**

LIVE SIMPLY. DREAM BIG. BE GRATEFUL. LAUGH LOTS.

CERTIFICATE OF WHOLENESS

This certificate is presented to

Sign Your Name

*for having the courage to change your name and giving
yourself permission to be the Perfect, Whole and
Complete Being God created You to be!*

Presented by: Andrenee Boothe, CEO & Founder

I am Worthy

I now release any and all thoughts, beliefs and feelings about my life that are not in alignment with my Worthiness and surrender them to the Presence of God in me.

	OLD	NEW
THOUGHTS		
BELIEFS		
FEELINGS		
ACTIONS		
SUMMARY		

be worthy today

♥ **DATE**

♥ **SCHEDULE FOR TODAY**

1 ....

2 ....

3 ....

4 ....

5 ....

6 ....

♥ **THINGS TO DO**

♥ **NOTES**

LIVE SIMPLY. DREAM BIG. BE GRATEFUL. LAUGH LOTS.

ANDRENEE'S CORNER, LLC

CERTIFICATE OF WORTHINESS

This certificate is presented to

Sign Your Name

for having the courage to change your name and giving yourself permission to be the Worthy Being God created You to be!

Presented by: Andrenee Boothe, CEO & Founder

I am Excellence

I now release any and all thoughts, beliefs and feelings about my life that are not in alignment with my Excellence and surrender them to the Presence of God in me.

	OLD	NEW
THOUGHTS		
BELIEFS		
FEELINGS		
ACTIONS		
SUMMARY		

be excellent today

♥ **DATE**

♥ **SCHEDULE FOR TODAY**

1 ....

2 ....

3 ....

4 ....

5 ....

6 ....

♥ **THINGS TO DO**

♥ **NOTES**

LIVE SIMPLY. DREAM BIG. BE GRATEFUL. LAUGH LOTS.

ANDRENEE'S CORNER, LLC

CERTIFICATE OF EXCELLENCE

This certificate is presented to

Sign Your Name

for having the courage to change your name and giving yourself permission to be the Excellent Leader God created You to be!

Presented by: Andrenee Boothe, CEO & Founder

I am Love

I now release any and all thoughts, beliefs and feelings about my life that are not in alignment with Love and surrender them to the Presence of God in me.

	OLD	NEW
THOUGHTS		
BELIEFS		
FEELINGS		
ACTIONS		
SUMMARY		

be loving today

♥ **DATE**

♥ **SCHEDULE FOR TODAY**

1 ....

2 ....

3 ....

4 ....

5 ....

6 ....

♥ **THINGS TO DO**

♥ **NOTES**

LIVE SIMPLY. DREAM BIG. BE GRATEFUL. LAUGH LOTS.

ANDRENEE'S CORNER, LLC

CERTIFICATE OF COMPASSION

This certificate is presented to

Sign Your Name

for having the courage to change your name and giving
yourself permission to be the Loving Being God
created You to be!

Presented by: Andrenee Boothe, CEO & Founder

I am Abundant

I now release any and all thoughts, beliefs and feelings about my life that are not in alignment with my Abundance and surrender them to the Presence of God in me.

	OLD	NEW
THOUGHTS		
BELIEFS		
FEELINGS		
ACTIONS		
SUMMARY		

be abundant today

♥ **DATE**

♥ **SCHEDULE FOR TODAY**

1 ....

2 ....

3 ....

4 ....

5 ....

6 ....

♥ **THINGS TO DO**

♥ **NOTES**

LIVE SIMPLY. DREAM BIG. BE GRATEFUL. LAUGH LOTS.

ANDRENEE'S CORNER, LLC

CERTIFICATE OF PROSPERITY

This certificate is presented to

Sign Your Name

for having the courage to change your name and giving yourself permission to be the Abundant Being God created You to be!

Presented by: Andrenee Boothe, CEO & Founder

I am Brave

I now release any and all thoughts, beliefs and feelings about my life that are not in alignment with my Courage and surrender them to the Presence of God in me.

	OLD	NEW
THOUGHTS		
BELIEFS		
FEELINGS		
ACTIONS		
SUMMARY		

be brave today

♥ **DATE**

♥ **SCHEDULE FOR TODAY**

1 ....

2 ....

3 ....

4 ....

5 ....

6 ....

♥ **THINGS TO DO**

♥ **NOTES**

LIVE SIMPLY. DREAM BIG. BE GRATEFUL. LAUGH LOTS.

ANDRENEE'S CORNER, LLC

CERTIFICATE OF BRAVERY

This certificate is presented to

_____

Sign Your Name

for having the courage to change your name and giving yourself permission to be the Risk Taking Leader God created You to be!

Presented by: Andrenee Boothe, CEO & Founder

I am Daring

I now release any and all thoughts, beliefs and feelings about my life that are not in alignment with my Audaciousness and surrender them to the Presence of God in me.

	OLD	NEW
THOUGHTS		
BELIEFS		
FEELINGS		
ACTIONS		
SUMMARY		

be daring today

♥ DATE

♥ THINGS TO DO

♥ SCHEDULE FOR TODAY

1 ....

2 ....

3 ....

4 ....

5 ....

6 ....

♥ NOTES

LIVE SIMPLY. DREAM BIG. BE GRATEFUL. LAUGH LOTS.

ANDRENEE'S CORNER, LLC

CERTIFICATE OF BOLDNESS

This certificate is presented to

Sign Your Name

for having the courage to change your name and giving
yourself permission to be the Bold Leader God
created You to be!

Presented by: Andrenee Boothe, CEO & Founder

www.ingramcontent.com/pod-product-compliance
Lightning Source LLC
Chambersburg PA
CBHW062049090426
42740CB00016B/3067